KV-578-492

Written by David Holzer

Created by the Top That! team

TOP THAT! Kids™

Copyright © 2005 Top That! Publishing plc
Tide Mill Way, Woodbridge, Suffolk, IP12 1AP, UK
www.topthatpublishing.com
All rights reserved

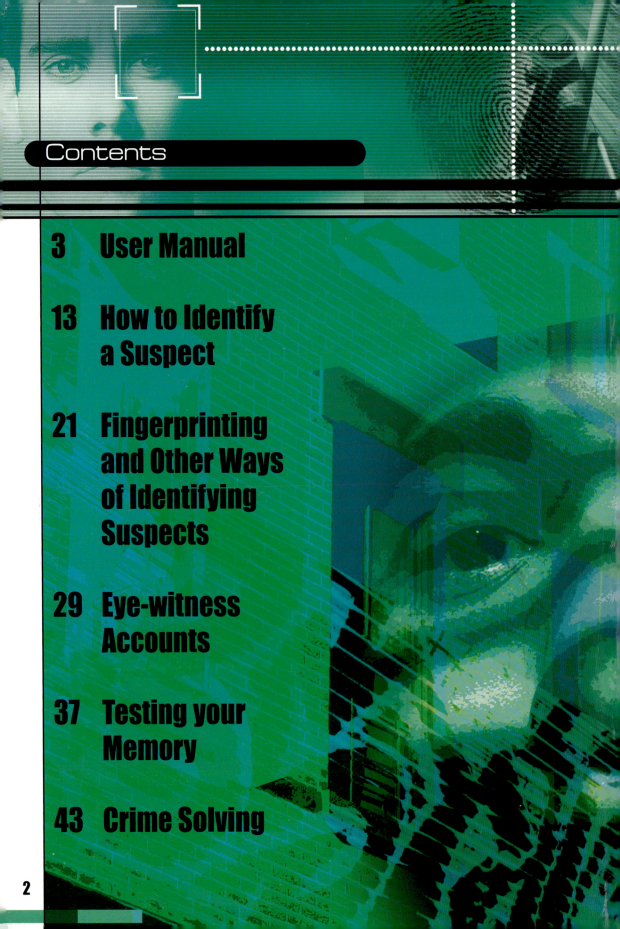

Contents

User Manual

This fun CD-ROM pack will help you learn how to solve crimes in the same way that real law enforcement agencies do. Discover how to create your own Identi-fit (electronic identikit™) faces to help you ID suspects and learn to identify and match fingerprints. Then you can create, and solve, amazing crimes using your imagination.

Running the CD

The Prime Suspect CD is easy to have fun with.

Using a PC

If you are using a PC, please double click on

primeSuspect-pc.exe

the 'my computer' icon on your desktop. Then click on the 'CD drive' icon and then on the file called primeSuspect-pc.exe.

Using a Macintosh

primeSuspect-mac

Double click on the 'CD' icon on the desktop and then double click on the file called primeSuspect-mac.

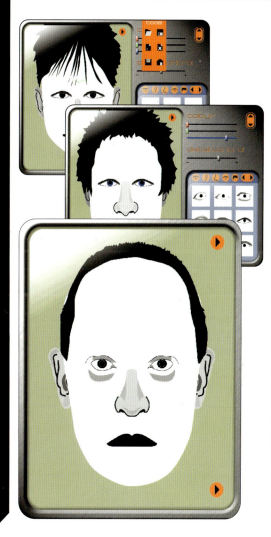

Minimum System Requirements

Before you use the CD-ROM, you will need to check that your computer is compatible – see below:

Screen resolution: 800 x 600
CD-ROM colour depth 32 bit (true colour)

PC users: Intel Pentium 166 processor running Windows TM 95/98 or NT version 4.0 or later, 64 MB of installed RAM, and a colour monitor.

Macintosh users: Power PC 120 Macintosh running system 8.1 or later, 64 MB of installed RAM, and a colour monitor.

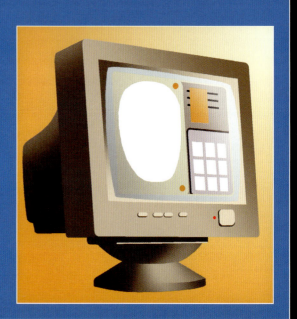

Printing the E-fits or fingerprints

Before you print any of the images from the CD-ROM, please check the printer settings under the 'File' menu and make sure you've selected 'quality paper'. You'll get the best results with thin, high-quality paper.

Any of the images will fill an A4 page. You should check that you have selected 'Portrait' under the 'Page Setup' menu.

You're nearly ready to start learning how to solve crimes. This easy step-by-step guide will tell you how to use the **CD-ROM** to create your own 'Identi-fit' faces and match fingerprints. There are also ideas for inventing your own crimes to solve.

Loading up

Once you've loaded and opened your CD, you'll see a 'Log-in' page. To log in to 'Prime Suspect' you'll need to use this secure passcode: PSTT03. Type it in then press the return key. Try to remember your passcode then no one will be able to spy on what you are doing.

Then just click on either 'Identi-fit' or 'Fingerprint', depending on which program you want to use.

The page

The page is the rectangle that appears to the left of the screen when you first open the program you're using. With 'Identi-fit' you'll see the outline of a face and with 'Fingerprints' you'll see a large fingerprint.

This is the only part of the screen that will print out and the place where you can add images taken from the databank on the right of the screen.

'Identi-fit' is an exciting way to create your own electronic identikit™ images, using methods that are much like those used by law enforcement experts to identify crime suspects. You have a choice of different-looking facial features – eyes, ears, nose, mouth and hair – and face shapes to use. Let's get started.

Creating a head outline

To build your 'Identi-fit' image start by choosing a head shape. On the blank page you'll see a head shape outline. Use the arrows at the top and bottom of the page to change the shape to how you want it.

After you have decided which head shape is right for your 'Identi-fit', decide what features you want to add to the face.

Choosing face parts

The menu of face features holds plenty of eyes, mouths, noses, ears, eyebrows and hairstyles for you to choose from when you're creating your 'Identi-fit'.

Look at the panel to the right of the face – each facial feature has its own icon which you can click on for a choice of features. The left and right arrows will help you scroll through the different panels. Select a part by double-clicking on it – it will appear on the head shape on the page.

To resize a facial feature, simply click on it and use the detail control slider to make it larger or smaller. To move the eyes closer together or further apart, hold down the shift key while the eyes are highlighted then use the detail control slider.

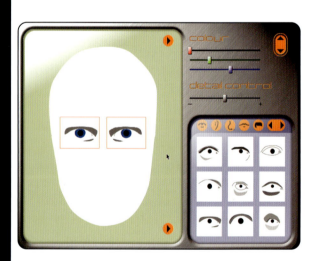

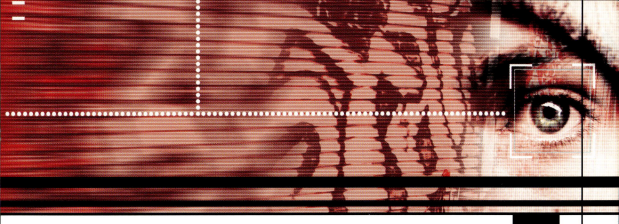

Removing a facial feature

If you want to delete a facial feature, highlight it first, then click on the arrows at the top right-hand side of the screen. The tool box will drop down. Clicking on the eraser icon will enable you to remove the facial feature you've selected.

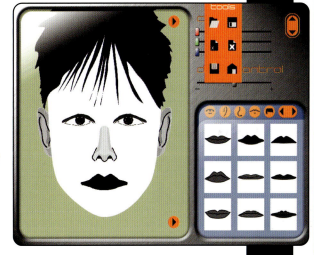

Adding or changing eye colour

With the suspect program, you can change the colour of the eyes you've chosen, to make your identikit™ look even more accurate.

When you've selected the eyes you want, use the three colour sliders to make them the right colour.

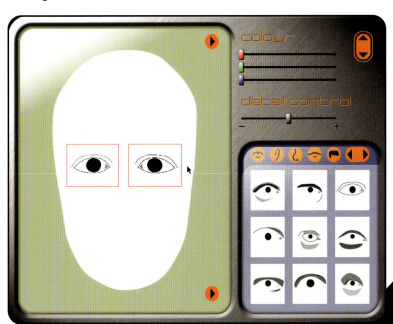

The tool box is the easy way for you to use 'Identi-fit'. Use the two arrows at the top right-hand side of the screen to display or hide the tool box. The bottom arrow makes the box drop down and the top hides it.

On the tool box you'll see these icons:

Main Menu
When you want to return to the main menu or get out of the program, click on this icon.

Erase
Use this icon when you want to remove any facial features you've chosen.

New Page
This icon will delete a whole face so that you can start again.

Print
Clicking on the print icon will print out your 'Identi-fit' in the shape of a proper 'Identi-fit' form as used by law enforcement agencies.

Save
You can save your work at any time by clicking on this icon. Give the file you've been working on a name that's easy to remember.

When you want to re-save a file, click on the icon again. You'll have to retype your file name in order to save it again. An alert box will then pop up, asking you whether you want to replace the original. Click 'Yes' if you have a PC or 'Replace' if you have a Macintosh.

If you want to keep your work top secret you might want to give the file a code name that only you know.

Open
Open a file by clicking on this icon.

Here are two fun ways you can use 'Identi-fit'.

The sneaky CD thief

Make up a crime. Someone in your family has been sneaking into your room and taking your CDs to play without permission, perhaps. Other members of your family think they've seen the culprit but they're not sure.

Get a photograph of someone in your family – your brother or sister perhaps – or write descriptions of what they look like from your 'witnesses': eye colour, hair length and so on.

Then see if you can match what that person looks like as closely as possible, using your 'Identi-fit'. When you think you've got a good likeness, show the other members of your family and see if they can guess who it is.

You are the suspect

Take a photograph of your face or position a mirror next to your computer. Then, by studying what you see, try to make an 'Identi-fit' of your own face. Have fun imagining the kind of crime you would be accused of. A daring midnight raid on the refrigerator maybe?

The 'Fingerprints' program lets you have fun learning how to identify different fingerprints and how to solve a crime by matching them. As you have to look closely at each fingerprint in order to match it you'll also improve your powers of observation.

'Fingerprints' works in a way that is very like the sophisticated computer-based technology used by law enforcement agencies around the world. The only difference is that they have millions of sets of prints to search.

What you'll see first

When you click on 'Fingerprints' on the main menu, you'll go straight into the program. You'll see a large fingerprint on the main page area. Remember that this is the only part of the screen that will print out.

The fingerprint databank

You'll see a series of small images of fingerprints in a panel on the right. This is the 'fingerprint databank' and it contains the fingerprints you'll need to match against the larger print on the main page area.

There are three pages of fingerprints and you can scroll between them by using the arrows at the top left-hand corner of the databank.

Matching fingerprints

To match fingerprints from the databank with those found at your crime scene (main fingerprint), you need to look hard at the main fingerprint so that you can identify its key features. No two persons' fingerprints are ever the same and they're identified by sets of patterns, marks caused by scars, and so on.

Look closely at the fingerprint, then try to match it with one of the prints in the databank. When you see one that might be a match, click on it and drag it over to the fingerprint on the main menu.

If the fingerprint flashes red when you place the match on top of it, you haven't identified it correctly. Try again.

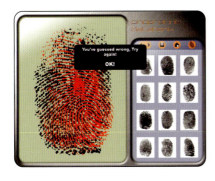

When you've dragged the correct print over, it will glow green and you'll read a message of congratulations. Press OK to get a new fingerprint.

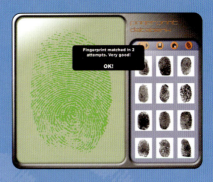

After you've successfully identified the fingerprint, you'll see a 'Searching' bar at the bottom of the main page. This means that the program is looking for a different fingerprint for you to identify.

The aim is to identify the criminal in as few attempts as possible.

Printing
When you want to print out a fingerprint, click on the print icon.

Home
When you want to get out of the 'Fingerprints' programme, or go back to the main menu, just click on the home icon.

As you know, the aim of 'Fingerprints' is to identify and match the correct fingerprint as quickly as possible. The better you get at the game, the closer you are to becoming a real detective.

You can play 'Fingerprints' with more than one person. Imagine a crime. Maybe one of you has secretly copied the other person's homework but has left a fingerprint at the scene of the crime. Or perhaps someone has borrowed your favourite computer game and lost it but left a fingerprint on the case.

Have fun using your imagination to make up an amazing crime.

The fingerprint on the main screen is the one that's been left at the scene of the crime. Take turns at the computer and see who can identify it first.

Good detectives know that there's always the possibility of human error when it comes to solving crimes. Witnesses are not necessarily one hundred per cent reliable. So, throughout history, law enforcement agencies have tried to come up with more and more scientific ways of proving a suspect committed a crime.

What is an Identikit™?

An Identikit™ is a scientific way of identifying suspects from descriptions given by victims or witnesses of a possible crime. Law enforcement officers work with witnesses using different head shapes and face parts to build up a picture of a suspect's face.

When an Identikit™, that looks as much like the suspect as possible, has been built up, it's given to all the witnesses to see if it matches the person they saw.

Identikit™ pictures also include details of how a person was dressed and any distinguishing features, such as tattoos, earrings or body height.

Some Identikits™ use photography to make them even more realistic.

The history of the Identikit™

The first person to be arrested using an Identikit™ picture was the French assassin

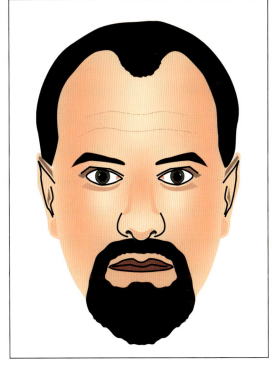

Guy Trebert. This took place in Paris, France, in 1959.

Identikits™ had been invented in America as a way of making police work more accurate and standardised. Before they were developed, law enforcement agencies employed artists who drew impressions of suspects based on what witnesses said.

This took a lot of time and wasn't necessarily very accurate. The Identikit™ changed all that.

Law enforcement agencies today use many different, clever ways of trying to identify suspects.

E-fits

Powerful computers mean that law enforcement agencies can create very good likenesses of suspects based on victim and witness statements. They can access thousands of different-looking facial features to build up a face – just like the CD-ROM 'Identi-fit' program.

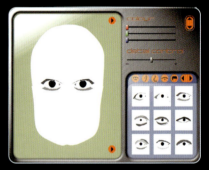

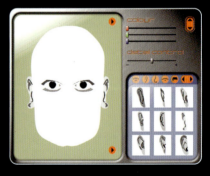

Computer drawing programs also allow them to redraw facial parts if they need to, so they're even more accurate and realistic. Once an image has been built up, it's called an 'E-fit', or electronic Identikit™.

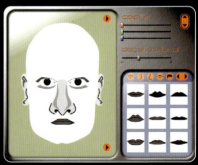

Closed Circuit Television (CCTV)

CCTV systems operate in most cities. They monitor buildings and roads. CCTV images can often help police to identify suspects and they record things, such as car number plates.

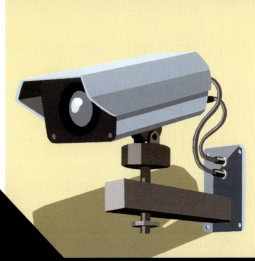

Photocalls

Whenever a person is arrested because he is suspected of committing a crime he has his photograph taken. Victims of crime and witnesses are shown photos of people who've been arrested on suspicion of committing similar crimes, in the same location. The police hope that this will lead to the identification of a suspect.

Police Lineups

When law enforcement agencies have arrested a suspect, they will often hold police lineups. They find a number of other people who look like the suspect and parade them, with the suspect, in front of witnesses.

If the same suspect is consistently picked out by the witnesses, there's a good chance he commited the crime.

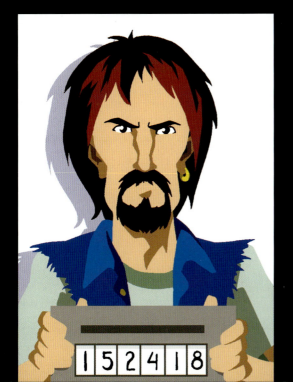

152418

Fingerprints and other types of physical evidence, such as DNA, are hard to come by at crime scenes and witnesses are not always able to provide the police with reliable statements. When police are unable to find much evidence and witnesses can't help with 'E-fits', photocalls, or lineups, the one piece of evidence police love to get is a confession from a suspect.

Through the years, interrogation techniques and psychological manipulations have become highly refined and are now used by police services across the world. Their success is undeniable and they have been used in the investigations of many crimes.

Police today use effective psychological methods to interrogate suspects and discover the truth.

Getting the Suspect to Talk

Psychological research has shown that people generally like others who are most similar to themselves in interests and beliefs. Accordingly, interrogators will initially pretend to have similar personalities and interests to the suspect – some even wear the same brand clothing as the suspect, if that can be determined in advance.

The interrogator may pretend to have an interest in some of the suspect's hobbies or in the suspect's lifestyle. By acting in such a manner, the interrogator leads the suspect to believe that he and the interrogator are similar in many ways.

This technique is meant to encourage the suspect to start talking. This is useful because once the suspect begins talking about any topic, it is harder for them to stop talking about other things, including crimes they may have committed.

Body Language

Trained interrogators can identify those who are deceptive in their answers. Firstly, they ask the suspect simple, non-stressful questions to get an idea of the suspect's normal behavior. The interrogator watches the subject's facial expressions and body language as they answer the questions. This is called kinesic interviewing. It gives the interrogator a very good idea of how the suspect acts when answering questions truthfully.

Neurolinguistic Interviewing

Interrogators can also use a technique called neurolinguistic interviewing which involves asking suspects two types of questions. One set of questions requires the suspect to remember data, and the other requires the suspect to think about problems. The interrogator then watches the suspect's body language to determine what type of changes take place when the suspect thinks of information, as opposed to remembering it.

Finally, when the suspect is asked questions directly related to the crime, the interrogator will be able to see if the suspect is thinking of lies to tell about a crime, or simply remembering the truth!

A confession from a suspect is a very valuable piece of evidence – even better than evidence from 'E-fits', photocalls or lineups.

You learned how the CD-ROM worked when you read the user manual.

Now that you know more about how 'E-fits' are used by law enforcement agencies, why not try using them to solve another crime that you've invented? This time, make things a little harder for yourself by having more than one suspect.

Think of a crime that involves more than one person – a bank robbery, for instance. Then make up three or four 'E-fits' by choosing the 'Identi-fit' option on the CD-ROM. Try to make them as different from each other, and as complicated, as you can.

You could even write down a description of the crime and turn it into a story.

Print out the 'E-fits' and then put them somewhere safe. Now see if you can recreate the 'E-fits' from memory. Try to do an 'E-fit' of every person who committed your imaginary crime.

When you've tried to recreate every single one, check them against your originals and see how close you were. Keep going until you get them right.

This will help develop your memory and your powers of observation.

Human memory is often unreliable. People can be absolutely convinced they've seen something – or be certain of a particular detail – only to find out that they were completely wrong. It's happened to all of us.

Here are some easy ways you can improve your reliability as a witness.

Remembering a face

Study a face. This can be anything from a photograph of someone famous to the real face of a member of your family. Write down what you can remember – the colour of the eyes, if they've got any distinguishing marks, and so on.

Then look at the photo again and see how much you've remembered correctly. Keep going until you've built up a completely accurate, detailed picture.

Being relaxed

Always be relaxed when you're trying to remember something – if you try too hard, or you get flustered, your memory doesn't work as well.

Memory exercises

Start to exercise your memory using simple tests.

For example, do you know what the number plate of your family car is? Try writing it down from memory. If you haven't got it right, keep practising.

Being able to memorise car number plates instantly is a handy skill for any detective.

Witness Statement Game

You can have great fun using law enforcement methods of obtaining witness statements to see if you can solve a crime.

Find a video or DVD that shows a crime being committed. If you can't find one, it doesn't matter, just use any piece of film. It can be from your favourite video.

Watch the piece of film as many times as you need until you memorise exactly what happens. Write down key things from the film – like the hero's or villain's hair colour, what they were wearing or the car they were driving.

Write ten questions that tie in with what is on the piece of film. For example:

- What colour eyes does the hero have?

- What does the bad guy say when he attacks the hero?

- How much money are the criminals trying to steal?

- What is the number plate of the getaway car?

Ask your family or friends to watch the film. Then ask them the questions you've written and see if they can answer them from memory.

When they've finished, play the piece of film again and see how many questions they answered correctly. There's probably a big difference between what they thought they saw and what actually happened.

The game is great fun to play but it also shows why law enforcement agencies take care to get accurate witness statements.

Fingerprinting and Other Ways of Identifying Suspects

The fingerprints of every single person are unique to them. If fingerprints can be recovered from a crime scene and matched to a suspect's, they are a very accurate way of finding out who committed the crime. The police also use **DNA** and voice fingerprinting to help solve crimes.

Today, taking the fingerprints of a suspect and matching them to any fingerprints found at the scene of a crime is standard crime-solving procedure. A suspect's fingerprints are also matched against any others the law enforcement authority holds to see if they have committed other crimes for which they are yet to be caught.

The first people to use fingerprints as a way of identifying people were the Chinese and Assyrians, who used them for signing legal documents.

Modern fingerprinting begins

In 1823, Johannes Evangelista Purkinje, a Czech physiologist, developed a system of classifying fingerprints. His system never became popular.

Later on in the 19th century, the British scientist Sir Francis Galton suggested using fingerprints of all ten fingers to identify individuals.

The police discover fingerprinting

Fingerprinting as we know it today was first used by Sir Edward Richard Henry, a British police officer stationed in Bengal, India in the 1890s. When he moved to London in 1901 to join the Metropolitan Police, he established the first ever file of fingerprints.

For nearly one hundred years, fingerprints were the most accurate way of identifying possible crime suspects.

The FBI in the US have more than 250 million sets of fingerprints on file. This is the largest collection in the world and is used by law enforcement agencies globally to help solve crimes.

The problem with fingerprints

When you watch a film or television show, or read a book, what is the first thing a criminal committing a crime usually does? He puts on gloves.

Like all of us, criminals are well aware that they can be identified by their fingerprints. However, if a criminal has been careless, law enforcement authorities can still find a print, even if it's what they call a 'partial'.

A 'partial' is part of a fingerprint. If law enforcement authorities are lucky it still might provide enough information to identify a suspect.

Criminals know all about fingerprints but scientists have now developed other ways of identifying suspects. These are also used by law enforcement agencies.

They include DNA fingerprinting, voice recognition, iris scanning and other methods which are making it a much riskier business to be a criminal. Learn more about these other methods on pages 27–28.

What is a Fingerprint?

Up until recently, fingerprints were the only way to identify any one of us because our fingerprints are unique to us. No two people, not even identical twins, have the same fingerprints.

Fingerprints are created by the tiny ridges of skin that form on the underside of our fingertips.

There are three types of fingerprint pattern – horseshoe, spiral and arch.

Spiral

Horseshoe

Arch

Although our fingerprints are unique to us – and stay exactly the same throughout our lives – they belong to one of these three categories.

If we have particularly noticeable scars on any of our fingerprints, this makes them even easier to distinguish.

When law enforcement agencies discovered that fingerprints were unique the next thing was to learn how to recover them from the scene of a crime.

They realised that any smooth, hard surface that has been touched by the human hand holds fingerprints because our skin secretes oil, which leaves a mark. This is called a latent print.

By using highly refined powder, or treating the surface of objects or weapons that have been found near a crime scene, detectives are able to recover the latent print. The latent print is then photographed or preserved in some other way.

Law enforcement forensic experts, who are specially trained to handle evidence carefully – including fingerprints – try to figure out what happened and then match the print against their records.

Preserving the crime scene

Latent prints can easily be destroyed by other people touching surfaces or objects. So it's essential for law enforcement agencies to make sure that a crime scene is not disturbed.

This is why, if you see a crime scene on television or in a film, it has usually been sealed off with bright yellow tape so no one, apart from the police, can get in.

It's also why you see detectives wearing gloves when they enter a crime scene. The last thing they want to do is leave their own fingerprints anywhere.

Whenever someone is arrested on suspicion of committing a crime, their fingerprints are taken.

Police officers who are specially trained to take clear sets of fingerprints roll all ten fingers in ink. They then take prints by placing the person's fingertips on a surface that will take a clear print and which won't fade.

What happens to the fingerprints?

The suspect's fingerprints are then kept on file, sorted according to which of the three types of pattern – spiral, horseshoe or arch – they fall into.

Today, whenever a law enforcement agency arrests a person who is suspected of committing a crime they digitise their fingerprint records. They do this by electronically scanning the original fingerprint, which was recorded in ink.

Digitising fingerprints

Digitising is a way of recording information electronically so that it can be stored on computers and 'read' by other computers. All of the information on the CD-ROM and this book has been created using digitisation.

Millions of sets of fingerprints across the world have been digitised and stored on computers. When a person is arrested because he or she is suspected of committing a crime, law enforcement officers can check his or her fingerprints against other fingerprints that belong to the same type of pattern.

This means that even if he or she didn't commit the crime he or she is being accused of, he or she could be arrested on suspicion of committing another.

You learned how to use the CD-ROM to match fingerprints at the beginning of this book. Now that you've learned more about how real law enforcement agencies use fingerprinting to help catch suspects, why not try something a bit more difficult?

Invent an imaginary crime and write it down like a story. It could go something like this… Some criminals broke into a luxury apartment, disabled the alarm system and stole valuable jewellery. Expert criminals, they wore gloves and didn't leave any fingerprints… or so they thought.

One of the criminals tore his or her glove at the finger when he or she was forcing open a window. He or she was being careful but has left a partial print which, if you're clever, you should be able to identify.

When you see the fingerprint which the 'Fingerprints' program wants you to identify, print it out and cover up part of the print. You'll then have the equivalent of a partial print, which will be much harder for you to identify.

You can keep practising your skills this way by printing out fingerprints and covering up different parts of them, making it harder and harder for yourself.

DNA Fingerprinting

Deoxyribonucleic acid (DNA) is a genetic blueprint found in the double strand of molecules called chromosomes found in the cell nuclei of all living beings.

Apart from identical twins, every single person's DNA is unique. DNA fingerprinting was developed to help understand the causes of genetically inherited diseases.

It was first used in a criminal investigation around 1985. More and more law enforcement authorities are now using it to help establish who committed – or didn't commit – a crime.

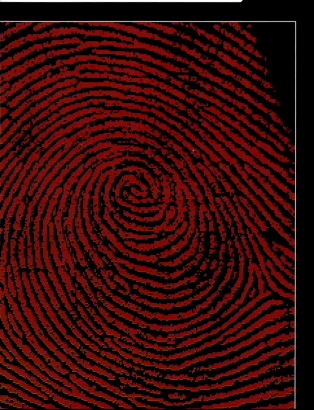

How to obtain a DNA fingerprint

DNA is usually extracted from body tissue or fluid like blood or saliva. Parts of DNA that can distinguish one individual from another are segmented and arranged. Probes mark the segments. X-ray film is placed on the probes and developed to form a pattern of black bars – the DNA fingerprint. DNA fingerprints are then compared for similarity.

What is DNA fingerprinting used for?

It is used to compare a sample of body fluid or tissue found at the scene of a crime with that of a suspect's. DNA fingerprinting can also be used to prove that a person suspected of a crime is innocent.

Crimes that occurred before DNA fingerprinting was developed have now been solved. People accused of committing crimes years ago have now been proven guilty or sometimes, innocent.

Iris identification

The iris is the coloured portion around the pupil in your eye. Our irises are all different and sophisticated machines have been developed that record the details of our irises to enable us to be identified by them.

Graphology

Graphology is the detailed study of a person's handwriting to see what it reveals about them. It can also be applied to documents – to find out if they're forgeries, for instance.

Speech and voiceprint recognition

Some computers can recognise a number of spoken words and this can then be used to identify if a particular person is speaking.

Voiceprinting is often used by the police to try to identify criminals who make obscene or threatening phone calls.

It works on the same principle as fingerprinting because the physical characteristics that make the sound of our voice are not exactly the same in any two people.

The examples on the following pages will give you an idea of how detectives might use eye-witness accounts and evidence to build up a picture of a crime. Use the 'Identi-fit' program to create a picture of the suspect or suspects in each case. When you've read the eye-witness accounts, try inventing some of your own.

Turn to page 35 for the answers.

The Burglary

A priceless painting is stolen from an art gallery. It has been protected using state of the art alarm and surveillance systems but the burglar still managed to steal it.

The police discover a security guard's uniform stuffed in a rubbish bin near the art gallery. Although they couldn't find any fingerprints on the picture frame, they find a clear print on the shiny peak of the guard's cap.

> Once you have read all the evidence, try building an 'E-fit' based on the eye-witness accounts. You might want to print it out and add details like the moustache and do a sketch showing how tall the burglar was.

Whoever the guard was, they had to take off their gloves to avoid looking suspicious but forgot to wipe the shiny peak clean.

You have three eye-witness accounts to use to build up an 'E-fit'.

Mr A

Mr A worked with the security guard, who joined only a few weeks before. He describes the missing guard as having bulging eyes that are very far apart, a small nose, big ears and dark hair.

Ms B

Ms B works in the art gallery café and the missing security guard liked to talk to her. She describes him as having: light blue eyes, short hair and a thin face.

Mrs C

Mrs C is a schoolteacher who was taking a party of children around the museum. She saw the security guard running away and says he had a small mouth and a pale complexion. She says he was also very tall.

A car was involved in an accident. No one was hurt but the driver drove away without stopping. Several people saw the driver and were able to give the police a description.

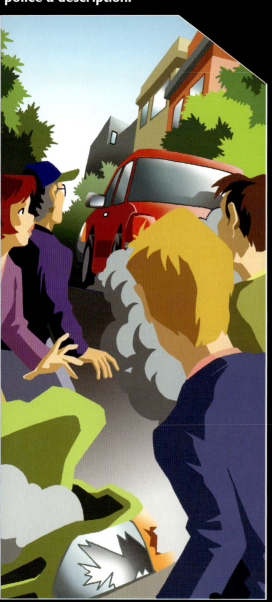

Witness A

Witness A said the driver had a very big head, small, narrow eyes, no hair and big ears.

Witness B

Witness B also said that the driver had a very big head, no hair and small, narrow eyes. But she said that he had normal-sized ears.

Witness C

Witness C agreed that the driver had normal-sized ears but not that he had a big head or was bald. She said that he had short hair, small, narrow eyes, a normal-sized head and very green eyes.

Witness D

Witness D agreed with Witness C that the driver had short hair and small, narrow eyes but also with A and B that he had a very big head and no hair. He added that the driver had a big nose.

Now create an 'E-fit' based on the various different eye-witness accounts. You need to decide what to do about the accounts that aren't the same.

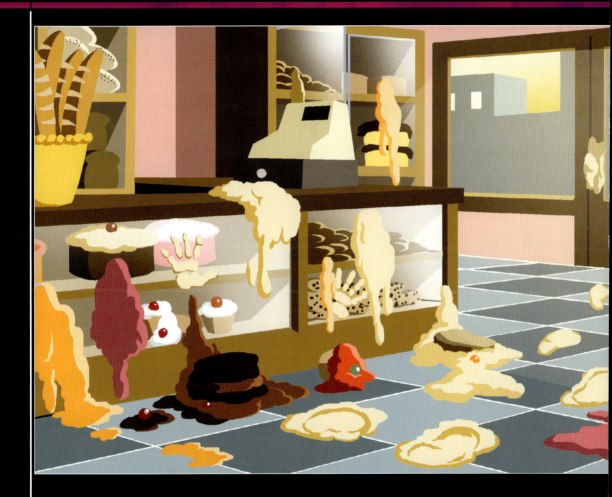

The bakery has been broken into. Nothing has been taken but there are cakes everywhere. This means that there are plenty of fingerprints, as well as footprints, on the messy floor.

It seems that the bakery was broken into first thing in the morning because the milkman saw someone running away.

He describes the suspect as a very thin boy of around ten years old with short hair, big green eyes, a long, wide nose and small ears.

Now create an 'E-fit'. You might want to do a drawing of the boy showing his body as well as his face.

The Mystery Caller

Several people on one street have told the police that they were visited by someone who tried to find an excuse to get into their house. There are several descriptions so the police have a lot to go on.

Mr B

The suspect had long hair, small eyes that were wide apart and a bent nose.

Mr B also thought that the suspect had a blue jacket as well as red trainers.

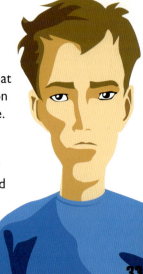

Mrs A

The suspect had long hair, nasty-looking eyes and a thin, long face.

He wore a dirty jacket that she thought was blue.

Ms C

Ms C says the suspect had small, blue nasty-looking eyes and a wide mouth.

The suspect also looked very haggard and tired.

Mr D

Mr D agreed with the others about how the suspect looked and dressed but he added that the suspect had a scar on the left cheek of his face.

Now create an 'E-fit'. You'll need to read over the witness accounts and build an impression from what you have been told.

The Skateboard Thieves

Someone has been stealing skateboards in the neighbourhood. At one house, where he broke in to steal the skateboard, he left a fingerprint where he had knocked over a tin of paint.

A little girl saw the skateboard thief skating away from a house. He was going very fast but she got a good look at him because he stopped to catch his breath back outside her house.

The witness said that the skateboard thief had long hair, big green eyes that were close together, a thin face and a narrow nose. She also noticed that he had spots and an earring.

Now make an 'E-fit'. You'll need to print it out to add the extra detail.

What the suspects could possibly look like...

The Burglary – p30

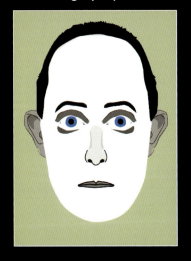

The Car Crash – p31

The Bakery Break in – p32

The Mystery Caller – p33

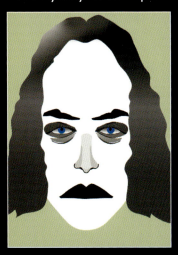

The Skateboard Thieves – p34

While it is always possible that a witness is wrong, interviewing them is usually a reliable way of building up an image of a suspect.

In the Case of the Car Crash, the above Identikit™ has been put together by taking the most common answers given by witnesses.

A gang has been spending counterfeit (fake) money in shops in the town. They hand over banknotes with a large value, although these are not large enough to attract suspicion at the time.

There are four members of the gang and four shopkeepers have been able to provide eye-witness accounts.

Witness A describes suspect A

Suspect A is a woman. She has long hair, pretty blue eyes, a small nose and a round face.

Witness B describes suspect B

Suspect B is a young man. He has very close-cropped hair, large blue eyes that are close together, a big nose, a long, thin face and small ears.

Witness C describes suspect C

Suspect C is a fat old man. He has a small, fat face, small eyes, that are wide apart, a small nose and long hair.

Witness D describes suspect D

Suspect D is another young man. He has medium-length hair, wide-set brown eyes, a big, bent nose and large ears.

Now create 'E-fits' of the suspects.

Testing your Memory

If you're going to be a good detective you need to be very observant and have a good memory. You'll have fun playing the games on these pages but you'll also be training your powers of observation and improving your memory at the same time.

Identifying the correct objects

Study these objects closely, then turn over the page and answer the questions.

Now answer these questions

See if you can answer these questions without cheating by turning the page over if you don't know the answer.

Keep playing the game until you get all the questions right. It will really help improve your memory.

1. What colour was the car?

2. Which object was between the gun and the fingerprint?

3. Were the handcuffs locked or open?

4. In which ear did the man in the Identikit™ picture have an earring?

5. How many rungs were there on the ladder?

6. What were the values of the money?

7. What was the number on the car number plate?

8. Was the fingerprint horseshoe, arch or spiral?

Study this Picture

Spend as long as you like studying this picture. Notice all the details. Make notes if you need to. Questions to test your memory are on page 42.

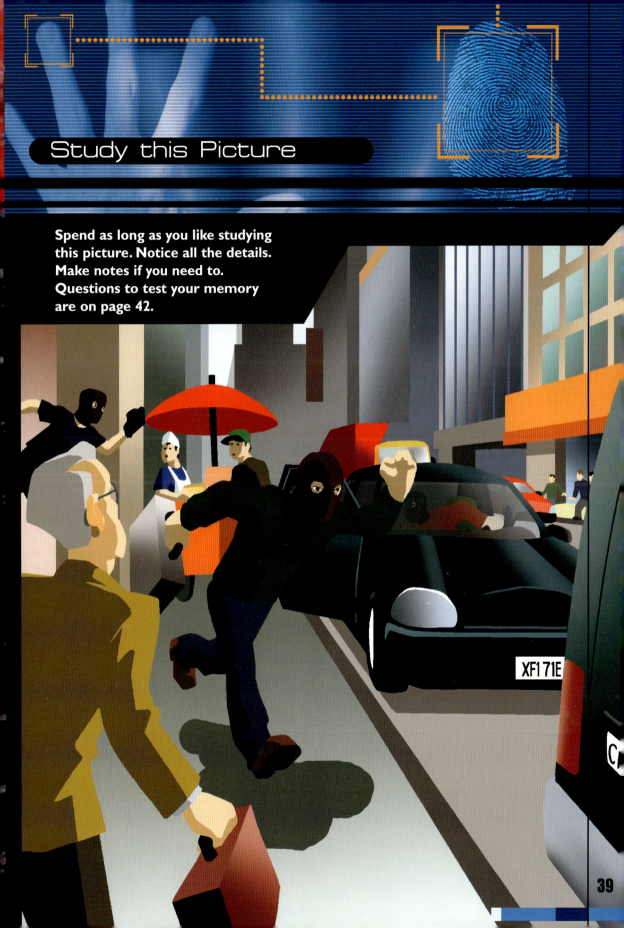

Look very closely at these two pictures. They look the same but they're not. When you really study them you'll notice plenty of differences.

Write down all the differences you can see. Try not to draw on the page or you won't be able to play the game again.

Now turn to page 42 to see how many differences you should have spotted.

The 'Change Your Appearance' Game

This game is great fun but you need to be very observant. You play it with two people.

The two of you stand facing each other and look at each other very closely for one minute.

Then you turn your backs to each other and change something about your appearance.

You might put your t-shirt on back to front, mess up your hair or pull one of your socks down. Anything you can think of.

Turn around and face each other again and try to spot what the other person has done to change his or her appearance. When you have either spotted the difference or given up, try again. Keep going until you've run out of ideas.

Answers to spot the difference on page 40

How many differences did you spot?

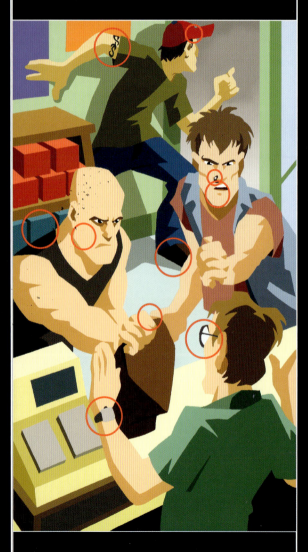

Remember the picture on page 39? Did you study it closely enough to know the answers to these questions?

1. How many cars are there in the picture?

2. What color are the shoes of the man with the green jumper?

3. How many men are there in the picture?

4. What is the number plate of the van?

5. What colour is the van?

6. Where is the man wearing the green cap standing?

7. What is the number plate of the car?

8. How may people can be seen on the far side of the road?

9. What is the old man in the foreground holding in his right hand?

10. Which letter can be clearly seen at the top of the picture?

Crime Solving

On the next few pages you'll find descriptions of crimes that have been committed. They can be solved using some of the methods we've talked about:

Fingerprinting

Graphology – analysing handwriting

Creating an Identikit™ picture

Fibre analysis

When you've read the story of the crime, take a few minutes to try to decide what you think happened.

The solution to each crime is revealed when you turn the book upside down. Be warned, the answer isn't always what you thought it was going to be.

Who Ate It?

It's Sunday morning and Grandma is coming for lunch. This is a special occasion as she lives a long way away.

Chicken is Grandma's favourite food and Mum has cooked a huge one, using Grandma's favourite recipe. Before lunch, she takes it out and leaves it to cool in the breeze which was gently blowing into the kitchen through the open french doors looking onto the garden.

Grandma arrives and everyone greets her, including the family dog. Then everyone sits down to lunch, waiting for Mum to appear with the chicken and for Dad to carve it. A cry of shock comes from the kitchen and the family rush out to see what's happened. The chicken has gone.

You start by looking for fingerprints. There should be plenty because chicken is very greasy. You find three sets and match them against members of the family. They belong to Mum, Dad and your sister. Your dad admits to tearing off a bit of meat and your sister has sneaked a piece of stuffing. Mum was the cook so it makes sense that her fingerprints were there.

Then you find a suspicious looking hair on the floor. You examine it and realise that it isn't human.

What happened?

Turn the book upside down to find out what happened.

The answer:
Your dog leapt up onto the table and ran out through the open French doors into the garden, where it ate the chicken.

The Broken Flowerpot

Mum's favourite flowerpot, which she was given as an anniversary present by Dad, is kept out on the back porch. In it she keeps her favourite flowers.

One morning, after a very cold frost, Mum goes out onto the back porch to do some gardening and notices that her favourite flowerpot is broken. The flowerpot is situated underneath the icy porch roof. She's very angry and decides that one of her children must have broken the flowerpot and not told her.

She looks at the garden but there are no footprints. There are also no tyre marks on the porch which would have suggested that someone was riding a bike where they shouldn't have been. There is a small puddle of water close by.

All of her children deny that they broke the flowerpot and they all have an alibi for where they were the day before.

What happened?

Turn the book upside down to find out what happened.

The answer:
Because it had been so cold, icicles had formed on the underside of the porch roof. One particularly big icicle had formed over Mum's flowerpot. When the sun came up that morning it had partly melted the huge icicle which had then crashed on to the flowerpot, knocking it over and smashing it. The only clue to what happened was the small puddle, caused when the icicle melted.

It is February 14th. When the post arrives, in the middle is a card with no stamp. It is addressed to your sister.

Your sister thinks her Valentine's card is from one of two boys she knows. From the information gathered from your neighbours and family, you decide to put together an Identi-fit to find out who it was.

Your sister said Boy A has large eyes, dark hair and thin lips. Boy B has blond hair, small eyes which are quite close together, and big lips.

You show your neighbour the two identi-fits, but she says she saw neither boy in your street that morning.

However, your friend from the end of the street says she had seen boy A chatting to the postman that morning.

What happened?

Who sent your sister's Valentine, and how? Turn the book upside down to find out.

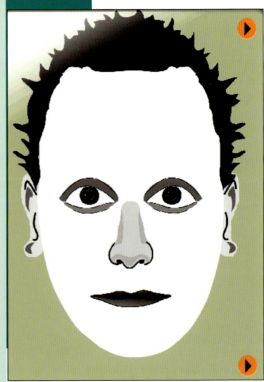

The answer:
Boy A sent the Valentine. To avoid being seen, he asked the postman at the end of the street to slip it into your post that morning.

Gnome Place Like Home

Mrs Jenkins, an old lady who lives on your street, asks for your help in solving a mystery.

Mrs Jenkins' garden gnome disappeared several months ago and, ever since then, she's been getting photographs from all over the world showing the gnome next to famous landmarks. There is writing on the photographs that is meant to be from the gnome, saying he's having a great time.

Mrs Jenkins is not angry. She thinks it's funny. But she would really like to know who has played the joke on her.

The handwriting on the photographs is all the same. It looks familiar to you but, at the same time, slightly strange.

You go around to your friend Susie's to tell her about the mystery. When you go around to the back of her house, you see Mrs Jenkins' garden gnome in her backyard.

Then you see Susie's brother Michael using his computer. You look over his shoulder to see what he's doing. He's making up pictures by combining different ones together. You notice his handwriting on his homework. It's nearly the same as the writing on the photographs.

What happened?

Turn the book upside down to find out what happened.

The answer:
Michael, who is very good with computers, had stolen the gnome and combined photographs of it with those of famous landmarks around the world. He had sent them to Mrs Jenkins, writing the message using the hand he doesn't normally write with to disguise his handwriting.

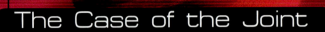

The Case of the Joint

Someone smashed a glass pane on your back door to let themselves into your house. Nothing has been taken. There are no fingerprints. Unusually, Dad is not angry and doesn't want to take things any further.

Dad seems very vague about where he has left his back door key and thought perhaps he may have to have a new one made. You decide to investigate.

First of all, you find something mysterious-looking that is attached to a piece of broken glass. It's flesh, but it isn't human.

Your mum says that you're having lamb for dinner. She's got a nice joint in the freezer, which is out in the garage, that needs eating up. Your dad, who normally loves lamb, says he isn't very hungry and would rather have something different for a change.

Dad's behaviour gives you an important clue to what happened.

What happened?

Turn the book upside down to find out what happened.

The answer:
Dad had come home and realized that he'd left his back door key at work. No one was home and he really needed to get into the house. He found the key to the garage, which was kept under the flowerpot, opened the freezer, found the leg of lamb and smashed the window with it.

He was too embarrassed to tell Mum what he'd done so used the microwave oven to defrost and cook the leg of lamb, before eating the evidence!